Symphony by the Fire

Symphony bythe Fire

A Book of Poetry

Judith Ansley

SYMPHONY BY THE FIRE
A BOOK OF POETRY

Copyright © 2016 Judith Ansley

ISBN-13: 978-1540473936

Email the author: ja.author4@gmail.com

CONTENTS

INTRODUCTION

People express themselves in many different ways, through music, dance, and other arts. Even as a young girl, I loved the arts—drawing, clay making, poetry, and more. While I have drifted away from drawing and clay making, poetry has always remained within me.

Symphony by the Fire was written to express how I see life and love. As poets, we tend to see things differently from most people. All of the poems in this book were born from my own life and love experiences, yet poetry speaks to us all in its own special way.

I want my poetry to encourage you to think about the meaning of life. Consider your own experiences with love, and be empowered instead of victimized. Many people do not learn, accept, or grow from their own mistakes when it comes to relationships and life choices.

There are many lessons to be learned from life and love combined, and so, I hope you will be inspired and uplifted, as you read my second published book, *Symphony by the Fire.*

A Painter's Brush

He was charming and intriguing.
His soul was mystic blue.
As I painted him, I realized
he looked good in any hue.

As I washed his feet with lavender,
as I kissed his lips of gold,
my mind created a fantasy
my heart could never hold.

I laid colors on top of colors,
mixing pink with sandy brown.
Though my painter's brush was tainted,
I still painted him a crown.

With every stroke of color
and with every dash of art,
my masterpiece then crumbled,
and broken was my heart.

Today, I'll Live

Today, I'll live.
I'll run to the light.
I am happy this time.
My spirit is alive.

Today, I'll live,
kiss the past good-night.
It doesn't matter the mistake;
the lesson is mine.

So after it's all over,
stamped and sealed,
God made a way
for something so real.

Today has come.
Today, I'll live.

Love's Departure
Part 1

The last time she was abandoned by love,
she found a letter written for good-bye.
Calligraphy danced across the paper,
but this time, she didn't cry.

This time, she'll wish love farewell
and await new love's return.
And when love writes her another letter,
next time, she'll just let it burn.

No more sonnets full of tears,
no more crying on her pillow.
No more being a victim of love,
no more weeping with the willow.

Her mother will be proud of the woman she became.
Finally accepting the truth that love will never change.

Burning This Letter
Part 2

Flames trickle down
the side of broken words.
Burning this letter
is less than what you deserve.

The mirage fell away
and your truth was revealed.
The smoke from your empty heart
was no longer concealed.

Fiery orange flames
burn so bright.
I sit back in awe
as I burn this letter tonight...

Anger

Let it grow,
let it enrage.
Let it turn
another page.

Let it speak,
let it live.
Let it take
all that you give.

Let it break,
let it bend.
Let it hate,
let it mend.

Let it crush,
let it scream.
Let it wake you
from a dream.

Let it hurt,
let it go.
Let it hide,
let it show.

Let it fuss,
let it know.
It will reap,
so let it sow.

The Enemy

I was attacked with every blade,
every weapon of possible destruction.
You couldn't pull me out of the deepest ditch
with the strongest suction.

I couldn't see past their rage; I was defenseless.
Crossing the finish line had faded from my wish list.
It was over for me,
bound and consumed, by negativity.

I was fighting for my life against an enemy unseen.
I lacked the support that I needed to succeed.
I was heading north on an arrow called "just me."
As I lost momentum, the crowd yelled, "Just breathe."
From the outside, easy is what it must be.

But easy was far from the truth.
I was bound to these chains at the depths of my roots.

I caught a glimpse into the mirror
to see an unbearable sight.
It was my own two hands
wrapped around my own neck, so tight.

I was falling under fast, and no one even knew
that I was my own enemy; it wasn't even you.

God, Are You There?

It's hard to sleep at night
when I can't feel You near.
It's hard to see the light
when darkness reappears.

I need You in my life
as the sun brings the day.
I still need Your protection
when Satan invites me out to play.

Can You please remove the fog
that has abruptly clouded my vision?
My trials scream so loudly,
when You speak, it's hard to listen.

I search for You daily,
seems you're merely in the distance.
As the stars begin to fall,
I reach for You as they glisten...

Hurting You

I was hurting you,
though I didn't know.
Your proud demeanor
wouldn't let it show...

I could've comfort you
if I had known,
but you shut me out,
you cried alone.

How could you leave me clueless?
You knew I cared for you.
On your last dollar,
I would still be there for you.

In this cold world
I see no other man.
Happiness is you and I,
walking hand in hand.

I need to know right now,
"Will you let me in?"
You are more than just my love,
you are also my best friend.

For any pain I've caused you,
I apologize.
Remember that mistakes
are only lessons in disguise.

I was hurting you,
though I didn't know.
Your proud demeanor
wouldn't let it show...

Venom

I thought it was love that surrounded me—
like a needle it shot through my veins.
A description of your love would be,
a poison that drives you insane.

It flowed through every part of me,
it shredded to pieces, the heart of me.

Did he not know
it was joy he took?
My heart was the bait
and his hate was the hook.

Swindled by his sweetness,
tricked by his charms—
Someone, please,
sound the alarm!

Awaken me from this nightmare...

Deceived me so bittersweet,
now I feel obsolete.
Lifeless, loveless, and incomplete,
all presented to me as a venomous treat.

Yet, if it slithers like a snake
that is what it must be.
My love was my adversary
and venom, my defeat.

Ocean's Note

I cried...
The tears rolled down my face
and across my sheets.

I cried...
Rolling river lakes drained
what was left of me.

I cried...
Until the ocean opened up
and spoke to me.

He said, "Here, love."
It was a note to me.

It read…

"Dear Judith, lift up your head.
Fix your clothes and get out of bed.

You may be hurting now
but joy is on its way.
Laughter is on her journey
to bring you gifts today.

Peace is racing time,
though she's running a little late.
Love is riding first class
to lighten up your day.

As the view from your window
allows you to look out over the ocean.
The waves can rage so high,
be careful not to get lost in motion.

Remember the beauty of life;
it isn't promised to be perfect.
It was never meant to be easy,
but in the end, it will be worth it."

As the note came to a close,
I heard knocking on my door…
it was love, peace, and joy
—everything the note said, and more.

I may have cried an ocean of tears,
I may have lost all of my hope.
But God's plan is still in action,
He wrote it out in Ocean's Note.

A Chance

A chance to write, a chance to speak,
A chance of a lifetime,
but what does it really mean?

What about the chances that lie in between?
What do those chances all add up to be?

Each one leads to somewhere new.
Is a missed opportunity an invisible clue?
I'm confused!

To a road imperfect but perfectly put together,
piece by piece they fit,
yet changing with the weather.

What am I supposed to do?
Wait here for a chance to choose?

A choice, but really no choice at all.
Free, but my back is up against the wall.
So what is a chance? What's the point of it all?

"The two most important days in your life
are the day you are born,
and the day you find out why."

- Mark Twain

Caged Mind

They say, poetic justice.

It gives us the freedom to express our feelings,
but let's talk about real things.

Like these bars that shape the cage,
that consume the minds of us all,
the young and the aged.

Not mentioning the cost
or the loss
of unexpressed expression,
you speak as if chains were your only possession,
blocked, tied, and bound by depression.

Do you freely speak?

Or is the word freely used too freely?
Or do I say it over and over in hopes that it will free me?

Brick by brick, mortar by mortar, we are trapped!

They say, poetic justice.

But there is no justice in cell-bound words spoken,
laying our hearts on the table,
broken and open.

It is not justice when there is no key
to unlock the cuffs that have cuffed me. Enough, please!
If your mind is locked away, you are not free.

They say, poetic justice.

I say no, it is definitely not justice,
but I tend to falter and fall between.
Is this the truth for us all
or the truth for just me?

I Am Free

I am free,
like a bond-servant
who has escaped.

I can breathe.
I am set high
in a better place.

A taste for wine,
lingers on the edge
of my lips.

I am ready,
like a boat docked
before it ships.

I am the brand.
I am The One,
the influential.

I can see
the power in my
full potential.

I am unique,
like a blue cherry
that sits on top.

I am a queen,
arresting his heart
but I'm no cop.

I am me,
a woman
who can't be stopped.

I can be
the woman
that you are not.

I am free.

Let it snow, let it freeze.
Turn to ice the misery.
Let it go, let me breathe,
Cut these strings, *I am free.*

Collaboration

Terry Conyers and Judith Ansley

Ice Water

Subtle as a liquid poured into a container,
calming the nerves of thirsty entertainers.

As the smoke clears,
a solid form is created from within.
Many days and nights I sat melting
from the thoughts of sins.

Afraid to freeze alone,
for your love, I have yet to earn.
Still I yearn, pray, and moan
for the seed I planted in you, has yet to burn.

As the temperature rises like the summer,
the burden of being wanted,
no longer is my consumption.

Our flame would not ignite
I felt trapped in a water cage.
Falling hopelessly to the bottom,
drenched I soaked in water's rage.

My heart once held a burning love
that stretched to Heaven's skies.
Who knew a love rekindled
would be the start of our demise.

I tried to find the spark again
but Heaven closed her door.
Our love was gone, forever lost at sea,
and hate became our core.

THE BREAKDOWN

The Author's Explanation

Caged Mind

If heart-break, fear, anger, or any other negative emotion consumes your mind, then you are bound by negative emotions. During the time I was writing out of heartbreak, I realized I was not free.

Love's Departure

In the beginning of the poem, the woman realizes that love has left her current relationship. At the end of the poem, the word "love" has two different meanings. The first is love being the wrong man, who will never change, while the second is love being God, who will also never change.

(1 John 4:16, Malachi 3:6)

Burning This Letter

The letter in this poem has two meanings. Literally, it is a letter that a man wrote to a woman, a letter full of lies and promises that he never kept. In its metaphorical meaning the letter is symbolic of the man.

Anger

In this poem, I warn someone not to take action based on the feeling of anger. I give anger human traits and refer to anger as its own independent being.

The Enemy

The moment you choose to receive negative mindsets and opinions of others, is the moment you become your own enemy.

God, Are You There?

The falling stars symbolize obstacles that arise in life. "I reach for You as they glisten," symbolizes the hope I still have in Jesus Christ through trials.

Ocean's Note

The ocean takes on human form and gives me a note which turns out to be a message from God.

I Am Free

This poem is written to empower all women. Break free from whatever it is that has been holding you back. You are strong and you are unique.

Collaboration "Ice Water"

Terry Conyers wrote the first half of this poem and I wrote the second half. We are both poets who decided to bring our creative minds together. "Ice Water" is a fictional piece.

Romans 8:28

"And we know that all things work together for good to them that love God, to them who are the called according to his purpose."

Made in the USA
Columbia, SC
08 August 2022

64918526R00024